Copyright © 2023 by William R. Foster (Author)

All rights reserved. No part of this book may be reproduced or utilized in any form or by any means, electronic or mechanical, including photocopying, recording or by any information storage and retrieval system, without permission in writing from the publisher, except for brief quotations in critical articles or reviews.

The content of this book is based on various sources and is intended for educational and entertainment purposes only. While the author has made every effort to ensure the accuracy, completeness, and reliability of the information provided, the information may be subject to errors, omissions, or inaccuracies. Therefore, the author makes no warranties, express or implied, regarding the content of this book.

Readers are advised to seek the guidance of a licensed professional before attempting any techniques or actions outlined in this book. The author is not responsible for any losses, damages, or injuries that may arise from the use of information contained within. The information provided in this book is not intended to be a substitute for professional advice, and readers should not rely solely on the information presented.

By reading this book, readers acknowledge that the author is not providing legal, financial, medical, or professional advice. Any reliance on the information contained in this book is solely at the reader's own risk.

Thank you for selecting this book as a valuable source of knowledge and inspiration. Our aim is to provide you with insights and information that will enrich your understanding and enhance your personal growth. We appreciate your decision to embark on this journey of discovery with us, and we hope that this book will exceed your expectations and leave a lasting impact on your life.

Title: Shadows of Silver: Legends of the Track
Subtitle: Untold Stories of Exceptional Racehorses and Their Legacy

Series: Tales of the Turf: The Legacy of White and Grey
Author: William R. Foster

Table of Contents

Introduction 5
The Mystique of Silver Coats 5
In the Company of Icons 8
Horse Racing: A Tale as Old as Time 12

Chapter 1: Phar Lap (Australia, 1926-1932), Chestnut with a white blaze 16
Phar Lap's Early Life and Background 16
Rise to Fame and the 1930 Melbourne Cup Victory 19
The Iconic 1932 Agua Caliente Handicap Win 22
The Enduring Legacy of Australia's Greatest Racehorse ... 25

Chapter 2: Red Rum ((United Kingdom, 1965-1995), Bay (appeared grey due to fading of coat with age) 29
Red Rum's Unique Story and Origins 29
The Remarkable Grand National Wins 32
The Enduring Popularity of a Horse with a "Grey" Reputation 35
Red Rum's Impact on the Grand National 38

Chapter 3: Spectacular Bid (United States, 1976-1981), Grey 41
Spectacular Bid's Early Career and Promise 41
The 1979 Kentucky Derby and Preakness Stakes Wins 44
The Controversy and Aftermath of the Belmont Stakes 47
The Enduring Appeal of a Horse Destined for Greatness .. 50

Chapter 4: Kincsem ((Hungary, 1874-1887), Grey . 53
The Story of the Undefeated Hungarian Legend 53
Kincsem's Global Recognition and Unmatched Record 56
Kincsem's Legacy in Hungary and the Racing World 59

The Extraordinary Journey of a White-Coated Heroine.... 62
Chapter 5: Shadows in the Pantheon 65
Exploring the Presence and Significance of White and Grey-Coated Horses in Racing History 65
The Unique Challenges and Advantages of These Coat Colors 68
The Shared Characteristics of These Legendary Horses 71
Chapter 6: The Jockeys Behind the Legends 74
The Skilled Jockeys Who Rode These Legendary Horses to Victory 74
The Partnerships and Bonds Between Horse and Rider 77
The Moments of Triumph and Challenge Faced by Both ...80
Chapter 7: Records Broken, Hearts Touched 83
The Race Records and Achievements of These Legendary Horses 83
The Impact of Their Stories on Racing Enthusiasts and Beyond 86
The Continued Fascination with the 'Shadows of Silver'.... 89
Conclusion 92
The Enduring Legacy of White and Grey 92
The Power of Equine Stories 96
A Tribute to Legends 100
Wordbook 103
Supplementary Materials 106

Introduction
The Mystique of Silver Coats

In the world of horse racing, where grace and power entwine in a dance of breathtaking speed, a select group of equine athletes stands apart, their gleaming white and grey coats akin to ethereal specters on the track. These are the legendary racehorses who have worn the "shadows of silver," defying convention and capturing the hearts of racing enthusiasts worldwide.

Silver-coated racehorses are a rarity in the world of equine athletes. Their coats, as striking as they are, carry an air of mystique, evoking a sense of wonder and fascination. It is this mystique that beckons us to explore their stories, to peel back the layers of history and discover the extraordinary journeys of these remarkable horses.

To understand the mystique of silver coats, we must first acknowledge the tradition and symbolism woven into the fabric of horse racing. In this sport where heritage is revered, and each race carries the echoes of countless contests before, the appearance of a white or grey-coated horse is an anomaly that defies the norms. The conventional image of a champion racehorse is one of fiery chestnuts, glossy bays, or sleek blacks, their coats shimmering like polished gems. Silver coats, however, possess a magic all their own, for they are the unexpected stars, the enigmatic figures, and the embodiment of the unpredictable nature of racing itself.

The appeal of these rare coats lies not only in their striking aesthetics but also in the symbolism they carry. White, often associated with purity and transcendence, lends an air of otherworldly elegance to the horses that bear it. Grey, with its spectral transitions from dark to light, represents the passage of time and the inevitability of change. The symbolism of silver coats transcends the races they compete in, becoming a representation of hope, transformation, and enduring spirit.

The mystique of silver coats also extends to the challenges they present to the racing world. In a sport where every detail matters, these coats pose unique considerations for trainers and jockeys. Their care and maintenance, the strategies employed to manage their unique needs, and the strategies to race them effectively all add layers of complexity to their stories. Yet, it is precisely these challenges that make their victories all the more spectacular.

The stories of silver-coated racehorses are a testament to the enduring human fascination with the mysterious and the beautiful. They are stories of triumph against the odds, of races won and records shattered. They are tales of loyalty between horse and rider, of the dedication of trainers and the unwavering support of owners. But above all, they are stories of the timeless allure of the horse racing world, where tradition and innovation collide, and where the shadows of silver continue to captivate, inspire, and astound.

As we delve into the remarkable narratives of legendary racehorses with silver coats, we will uncover the secrets of their success, the challenges they overcame, and the indelible mark they left on the world of horse racing. These are the shadows of silver, and their mystique beckons us to join them on a journey of wonder and admiration for the enduring legacy they have created. In the chapters that follow, we will explore their lives, victories, and the profound impact they have had on the sport, all while basking in the glow of their enchanting silver coats.

In the Company of Icons

In the world of horse racing, where the thundering hooves of champions echo through time, there exists a select and revered company of icons. These are the legendary racehorses, each bearing the unmistakable silvery mantle that sets them apart as truly extraordinary. Their presence in the annals of horse racing history is not merely notable; it is iconic. In this chapter, we step into the illustrious company of these equine marvels, exploring their lives, their achievements, and the indelible mark they have left on the sport.

The term "icon" carries weight and significance. It denotes something or someone that transcends the ordinary, leaving an enduring impression on the collective consciousness. In the realm of horse racing, these silver-coated icons are not mere competitors; they are symbols of the sport's grandeur, the embodiment of dreams fulfilled, and the bringers of unforgettable moments etched into the hearts of fans.

As we embark on this journey in the company of icons, it becomes evident that these horses are more than athletes; they are cultural touchstones. They represent the spirit of determination, the essence of beauty, and the resonance of hope. Their stories resonate beyond the boundaries of racetracks, crossing oceans and generations. To understand their place in the pantheon of horse racing legends, we must first recognize the attributes that define them as icons.

Unprecedented Achievements: Iconic racehorses achieve feats that defy the norms and expectations of the sport. Whether it's a historic winning streak, a record-breaking performance, or a comeback story for the ages, their accomplishments are etched in the record books and in the collective memory of racing aficionados.

Endurance and Legacy: The legacy of an icon extends far beyond the years they spent on the track. Their influence lingers in the bloodlines of future champions, the inspiration they provide to new generations of horsemen and women, and the continued interest they generate in the sport. Their enduring legacies ensure their place in history's pages.

Cultural Impact: Icons are cultural touchstones, symbols of their era. They grace magazine covers, inspire artists, and even find their names embedded in the popular lexicon. They become part of the tapestry of the times in which they lived, influencing the broader culture.

Fan Loyalty: The following that iconic horses amass is not limited to horse racing enthusiasts. They garner a devoted fan base that transcends borders and backgrounds.

Fans travel far and wide to witness their feats, don their colors, and take part in the collective celebration of their victories.

Inspiration: Iconic horses inspire the human spirit. Their stories serve as a reminder of the heights that can be achieved with dedication, perseverance, and a touch of that intangible magic that sets them apart. They inspire dreams, hopes, and the pursuit of excellence.

In the chapters that follow, we will immerse ourselves in the life stories of such icons, tracing their humble beginnings, their meteoric rises to fame, and the moments that defined their careers. From the beloved Phar Lap, who carried the dreams of a nation on his back, to the indomitable Red Rum, a symbol of triumph over adversity, these horses have a profound and lasting impact on the sport and its followers.

As we explore their journeys, we will encounter the intricate web of connections that surrounds them. The trainers who nurtured their talents, the jockeys who guided them to glory, and the owners who believed in their potential all play pivotal roles in the narratives of these icons. Together, they form a unique partnership, an alliance of dedication and unwavering faith in the pursuit of excellence.

These silver-coated icons embody the heart and soul of horse racing, and their stories are a testament to the magic of the sport. Join us as we embark on a journey through time, where the company of these icons reminds us that in the world of horse racing, greatness knows no bounds, and the shadows of silver continue to cast a luminous glow upon the track.

Horse Racing: A Tale as Old as Time

Horse racing, a sport steeped in tradition and folklore, is a narrative that stretches back through the ages. Its roots can be traced to distant antiquity, where the bond between horse and rider, the thrill of competition, and the allure of speed have captivated the human imagination. In this chapter, we embark on a journey through time, exploring the rich history of horse racing, its evolution, and the enduring appeal that continues to draw us into its enchanting world.

The history of horse racing is a tapestry woven with threads of human ingenuity and passion. It spans centuries, continents, and cultures, revealing a story of unbroken continuity, innovation, and adaptation. From the ancient civilizations of Greece and Rome to the vast landscapes of the Arabian deserts, the legacy of horse racing is intertwined with the story of humanity itself.

Antiquity and Origins: Our tale begins in the cradle of civilization, where horse racing was not merely a sport but a symbol of power and prestige. In ancient Greece, horse racing events were a part of the Olympic Games, celebrating the grace and strength of the equine athletes. Similarly, the Roman Empire witnessed the emergence of chariot races in massive arenas, with the thundering hooves of horses stirring the hearts of spectators.

The Arabian Legacy: From the deserts of Arabia emerged the Arabian horse, a breed renowned for its endurance, elegance, and swiftness. These horses played a pivotal role in shaping the genetic stock of racehorses across the world, leaving an indelible mark on the sport.

Medieval Pageantry: The Middle Ages saw the emergence of jousting tournaments and equestrian competitions that showcased the bond between knights and their steeds. The pageantry of the medieval tournaments and festivals laid the groundwork for the more structured and regulated forms of horse racing that would follow.

The Birth of Modern Racing: The 17th century witnessed the birth of modern horse racing in Britain with the establishment of racecourses, rules, and governing bodies. The sport, as we know it today, began to take shape during this era, with organized races and the emergence of iconic venues such as Newmarket and Epsom Downs.

The Global Reach: Horse racing transcended borders and found its way to various corners of the world. In the United States, it evolved into a dynamic and diverse industry, encompassing a wide array of racing disciplines, from thoroughbred to quarter horse and standardbred racing. Similarly, in Australia, the Melbourne Cup became a cultural institution, drawing fans from all walks of life.

Innovations and Milestones: Throughout its history, horse racing has witnessed numerous innovations and milestones. From the introduction of the stopwatch to the development of photo-finish technology, these advancements have enhanced the sport's integrity and provided fans with new ways to engage with the races.

The Enduring Appeal: The allure of horse racing lies not only in its storied past but in its capacity to evolve and captivate new generations. It remains a sport that unites people from diverse backgrounds, forging a common bond based on a shared love for these magnificent animals and the thrill of competition.

As we delve deeper into the chapters that follow, we will witness how silver-coated racehorses have become an integral part of this age-old tale. They are the latest chapters in a narrative that has withstood the test of time, embodying the essence of history, heritage, and the magic of the racetrack.

In the company of these icons, we'll explore the ways in which horse racing has transformed, from ancient traditions to the modern spectacle we know today. We'll witness how it continues to enchant, excite, and inspire, proving that this timeless tale is far from reaching its final chapter. Join us as we journey through the centuries, where the shadows of silver take their place in the grand epic of horse racing, a tale as old as time.

Chapter 1: Phar Lap (Australia, 1926-1932), Chestnut with a white blaze

Phar Lap's Early Life and Background

To understand the remarkable journey of Phar Lap, we must first turn the pages of history back to the beginnings of this equine legend. Born in the heartland of Australian racing in 1926, Phar Lap's early life and background reveal the humble origins of a horse who would become an enduring symbol of excellence and tenacity in the world of horse racing.

Birth and Lineage: Phar Lap, whose name means "lightning" in Thai, was foaled on October 4, 1926, at Seadown Stud in Timaru, New Zealand. He was the product of humble parentage. His sire, Night Raid, was an unremarkable stallion, and his dam, Entreaty, was a mare of unproven pedigree. In this unassuming heritage, the story of Phar Lap's rise to greatness begins.

Early Challenges: From the very outset, Phar Lap faced adversity. As a foal, he was a weak and scrawny colt, with none of the muscular grace that would later define him. In his early years, he battled a series of ailments and illnesses that threatened to halt his progress. It was only through the dedicated care of trainer Harry Telford and owner David J.

Davis that the young colt's potential was recognized and nurtured.

The Telford Connection: Harry Telford, a master horseman and trainer, saw something special in the awkward and fragile Phar Lap. Under Telford's guidance, the colt began to develop both physically and mentally. Telford's unwavering belief in his horse and his patient approach to training laid the foundation for Phar Lap's remarkable transformation.

Phar Lap's Acquisition: In 1928, Phar Lap was sold to American businessman David J. Davis, who recognized the horse's potential and made the fateful decision to acquire him. This move marked a turning point in Phar Lap's life, as it placed him under the ownership of someone who shared Telford's vision of what the horse could become.

Transformation and Growth: Phar Lap's transformation from a sickly colt to a robust racehorse was a testament to the dedication of those around him. With the right care, nutrition, and training, he began to flourish. His chestnut coat, with a distinctive white blaze on his forehead, became an emblem of hope for a nation enduring the hardships of the Great Depression.

Early Races and Development: Phar Lap's early racing career was marked by modest success and a series of lessons learned. He began competing in less prestigious races, gaining experience and confidence. It was during these formative years that the horse's potential began to shine through, and he hinted at the greatness that lay ahead.

Rising Stardom: As Phar Lap matured, his performances on the racetrack drew increasing attention. The combination of his raw talent, a skilled jockey in Jack Baker, and the unwavering support of his trainer and owner propelled him into the limelight. The stage was set for his meteoric rise to fame and the enduring legacy that would follow.

Phar Lap's early life and background provide a fascinating backdrop to the extraordinary journey that lay ahead. It is a story of persistence, resilience, and the transformative power of belief and dedication. In the chapters to come, we will explore how this once-unremarkable colt would emerge as one of the most celebrated and beloved racehorses in the history of Australian racing.

Rise to Fame and the 1930 Melbourne Cup Victory

The tale of Phar Lap's ascent to fame is a story of grit, determination, and an unwavering spirit that captured the hearts of a nation. His journey from a scrawny and sickly colt to a symbol of hope and triumph reached its zenith with the iconic 1930 Melbourne Cup victory, a moment that etched his name into the annals of Australian horse racing history.

The Early Races: Phar Lap's rise to fame was gradual but relentless. In the early stages of his racing career, he was tested in minor races, where he displayed glimpses of his potential. His performances were marked by a combination of determination and bursts of speed, traits that would become his signature on the track.

Breakout Moments: The turning point came when Phar Lap won the AJC Derby in 1929. This victory was not only a demonstration of his growing prowess but also a revelation of his remarkable staying power. It marked the moment when the racing world began to take notice of the chestnut colt with the distinctive white blaze.

The Agua Caliente Handicap: While Phar Lap's success in Australia was undeniable, his quest for global recognition took him to the United States. In 1932, he competed in the prestigious Agua Caliente Handicap, an event that pitted him against some of the finest racehorses in the world. The race would prove to be a watershed moment in his career.

Preparation and Hurdles: The journey to the Melbourne Cup was not without its challenges. Phar Lap's preparation for the iconic race involved careful planning, adjustments in training, and the skillful management of a horse whose growing fame was accompanied by the pressures of expectation. His trainer Harry Telford and jockey Jim Pike were instrumental in ensuring that he was in peak condition for the Melbourne Cup.

The 1930 Melbourne Cup: On that fateful first Tuesday in November, 1930, Phar Lap strode onto the hallowed grounds of Flemington Racecourse. The Melbourne Cup, the most prestigious race in Australia, was the stage for his crowning moment. With a record-breaking crowd in attendance, the nation held its breath as the chestnut champion took his place among a field of talented competitors.

The Race that Stopped a Nation: The 1930 Melbourne Cup was more than a race; it was a cultural event that transcended sport. As the horses thundered down the track, the crowd erupted in a deafening roar. Phar Lap, carrying the hopes of a nation, surged forward with a breathtaking display of speed and stamina. With jockey Jim Pike urging him on, he crossed the finish line in a moment that would become etched in Australian history.

The Aftermath: Phar Lap's victory in the 1930 Melbourne Cup was more than just a win; it was a symbol of resilience and the triumph of the underdog. The nation celebrated, and his name became a household word. The horse's impact extended far beyond racing circles, making him a beloved figure in Australian culture.

The 1930 Melbourne Cup victory catapulted Phar Lap to international stardom. It was a moment that not only defined his legacy but also served as an inspiration during a challenging period in history. In the chapters that follow, we will delve deeper into the iconic Agua Caliente Handicap in the United States and explore the enduring legacy of Australia's greatest racehorse. The shadows of silver cast a brilliant glow on the track, and Phar Lap's journey exemplified the magic of horse racing.

The Iconic 1932 Agua Caliente Handicap Win

Phar Lap's journey to international acclaim and his legacy as one of the greatest racehorses of all time would be incomplete without delving into his legendary victory at the 1932 Agua Caliente Handicap. This historic race not only catapulted him to global stardom but also left an indelible mark on the world of horse racing. In this chapter, we explore the iconic 1932 Agua Caliente Handicap win, a moment that elevated Phar Lap to legendary status.

The Setting: The Agua Caliente Handicap, held at Agua Caliente Racetrack in Tijuana, Mexico, was one of the richest and most prestigious horse races of its time. With a purse of $100,000, it attracted top thoroughbreds from around the world. Phar Lap's entry into this high-stakes race signaled a significant moment in his career.

International Ambitions: Phar Lap's journey to the United States was driven by a desire for international recognition. While he was already a national hero in Australia, his owner David J. Davis and trainer Harry Telford believed that success in the Agua Caliente Handicap would solidify his reputation as a global racing icon.

Challenges and Preparations: Phar Lap's journey to the United States was not without its hurdles. The logistics of transporting a prized racehorse across continents were complex, and the horse had to acclimate to new surroundings and racing conditions. Trainer Telford and his team faced the formidable task of preparing Phar Lap for the race of a lifetime.

Phar Lap's Form: As race day approached, the racing world closely followed Phar Lap's form. His performances in Australia had been consistently outstanding, but the question remained: could he adapt to the American racing environment and defeat top-class competitors on foreign soil?

Race Day Drama: The 1932 Agua Caliente Handicap was more than just a horse race; it was a global spectacle. Racing enthusiasts and the curious alike flocked to the Mexican racetrack, drawn by the aura of Phar Lap and the opportunity to witness a sporting legend in action.

The Race Itself: As the field burst from the starting gates, Phar Lap's supporters held their collective breath. The 1932 Agua Caliente Handicap was a grueling test of stamina, and the pressure was immense. Jockey Billy Elliott, who rode Phar Lap to victory in the race, executed a masterful performance, showcasing the horse's ability to adapt and conquer new challenges.

Triumphant Finish: Phar Lap's victory in the Agua Caliente Handicap was nothing short of legendary. In a breathtaking display of speed and endurance, he surged ahead in the final stretch, leaving his competitors in the dust. His win was celebrated not only as a personal victory but as a triumph of the entire racing community and the enduring bond between horse and rider.

Legacy and Impact: Phar Lap's victory in the 1932 Agua Caliente Handicap not only solidified his status as a global racing sensation but also left a lasting impact on the sport. He became a symbol of international excellence and a testament to the indomitable spirit of the horse. His legacy continues to inspire generations of racing enthusiasts.

Return to Australia: Following his momentous win, Phar Lap returned to Australia a true hero. The shadows of silver had not only brought him international fame but had illuminated the path for future generations of Australian racehorses.

The iconic 1932 Agua Caliente Handicap win remains a pivotal chapter in the remarkable journey of Phar Lap. It epitomizes the magic of horse racing, where the pursuit of excellence transcends borders and captures the hearts of people worldwide. In the chapters that follow, we will further explore the enduring legacy of Australia's greatest racehorse and the profound impact of the "big red" on the world of horse racing.

The Enduring Legacy of Australia's Greatest Racehorse

Phar Lap, the chestnut colt with a distinctive white blaze, emerged as not only a racing legend but an enduring symbol of excellence, determination, and the unbreakable spirit of Australia. In this chapter, we explore the legacy of this remarkable racehorse and the profound and lasting impact he left on the world of horse racing, as well as the collective memory of a nation.

An Australian Icon: Phar Lap's legacy is deeply entwined with Australian identity. He was more than a racehorse; he was a national hero, a symbol of hope during the Great Depression, and a source of pride for a nation that had weathered economic hardships. His name became synonymous with resilience and the Australian spirit.

Racing Records and Achievements: Phar Lap's record-breaking performances on the track were central to his enduring legacy. He set numerous records and achieved feats that were unprecedented in Australian racing history. His wins, including the Melbourne Cup, AJC Derby, and the Agua Caliente Handicap, were etched into the annals of time, establishing him as one of the greatest racehorses to grace the sport.

Popularity and Fan Following: Phar Lap's racing career coincided with a period when horse racing was a beloved and widely followed sport in Australia. His popularity extended beyond the racing community, drawing fans from all walks of life. People flocked to racetracks to catch a glimpse of the "big red" in action, and his victories were celebrated with a fervor rarely seen in the sporting world.

The Power of Phar Lap: Phar Lap possessed an innate ability to capture the imagination of those who saw him. He was a horse that transcended the boundaries of the racetrack, leaving a lasting impression on anyone who witnessed his incredible speed and determination. His impact was not limited to Australia; it resonated with racing enthusiasts worldwide.

Phar Lap's International Journey: Phar Lap's sojourn to the United States, where he won the Agua Caliente Handicap, further solidified his status as an international icon. His victory in this prestigious race served as a testament to his adaptability and drew attention to the quality of Australian racing. It was a defining moment in his career and a source of immense pride for his home country.

The Enduring Bond: Phar Lap's partnership with his trainer Harry Telford, jockey Jim Pike, and owner David J.

Davis exemplified the enduring bond between horse and human. Their unwavering belief in the horse's potential and their dedication to his well-being were central to his success. The legacy of their partnership adds depth to the story of Phar Lap.

Beyond Racing: Phar Lap's legacy extended beyond the racetrack. He became a cultural phenomenon, inspiring books, films, songs, and works of art. His name and image were woven into the fabric of Australian culture, ensuring that his story would be passed down through generations.

The Phar Lap Museum: The establishment of the Phar Lap Museum in New Zealand and the National Museum of Australia in Canberra, where his preserved hide is on display, serve as tangible reminders of his enduring legacy. These museums pay homage to the horse's greatness and continue to educate and inspire visitors.

Inspiring Future Generations: Phar Lap's story continues to inspire new generations of horse racing enthusiasts. His legacy serves as a reminder of the magic of the sport, the power of perseverance, and the enduring bond between horse and rider.

Conclusion: Phar Lap, Australia's greatest racehorse, remains a shining beacon in the world of horse racing. His legacy endures as a symbol of excellence, resilience, and the unwavering spirit of a nation. In the chapters that follow, we will continue to explore the profound impact of the "big red" and the enduring fascination with the shadows of silver that continue to illuminate the world of horse racing.

Chapter 2: Red Rum ((United Kingdom, 1965-1995), Bay (appeared grey due to fading of coat with age)

Red Rum's Unique Story and Origins

Red Rum, a name that echoes through the annals of horse racing history, possesses a unique and captivating story that begins with his origins and early life. Born in 1965, Red Rum's remarkable journey from a modest pedigree to becoming one of the most celebrated steeplechasers of all time is a testament to his extraordinary character and the indomitable spirit that defines his legacy.

The Early Days: Red Rum was born on May 3, 1965, in Ireland, at Rossenarra Stud. His breeding was modest, with sire Quorum and dam Mared. It was an unassuming beginning for a horse that would later capture the hearts of racing enthusiasts worldwide.

Early Training and Racing: Red Rum's early training took place under the guidance of handler Ginger McCain, who recognized the horse's potential and resilience. His early races revealed a natural aptitude for jumping and the stamina required for the grueling steeplechase courses.

Facing Adversity: One of the defining moments in Red Rum's early life was his susceptibility to health issues, including debilitating foot problems. These challenges threatened his racing career, but the dedication of his trainer and the skilled care of farrier Tommy Smith played pivotal roles in helping the horse overcome these obstacles.

Grand National Aspirations: Red Rum's entry into the Grand National, one of the most prestigious steeplechase races in the world, was a pivotal point in his career. His first attempt in 1973 resulted in a thrilling second-place finish. This was only a prelude to the historic victories that would follow.

The Miracle of Aintree: Aintree Racecourse in Liverpool, England, became the stage for Red Rum's greatest triumphs. His unmatched affinity for the Grand National course and his extraordinary ability to handle the challenging fences established him as a true Aintree legend.

The Triple Crown of Grand Nationals: Red Rum's unique story includes an unprecedented achievement—the rare feat of winning three Grand National titles. His consecutive victories in 1973, 1974, and 1977 not only solidified his status as a racing great but also endeared him to the British public, who celebrated him as a national hero.

The Fading Bay: Red Rum's appearance added to his mystique. Despite being a bay in color, his coat began to fade with age, giving the impression of a grey horse. This distinctive feature contributed to his recognition and set him apart as a unique figure in the world of steeplechase racing.

The People's Horse: Red Rum's appeal extended far beyond the racing community. He became a beloved figure in British culture, drawing fans from all walks of life who admired his underdog spirit and his ability to conquer the Grand National course like no other.

Retirement and Enduring Legacy: Red Rum's retirement from racing marked the end of an era, but his legacy continued to grow. He became an ambassador for the sport, making public appearances and enjoying a well-deserved retirement. His name remains synonymous with the Grand National, and his story inspires both seasoned racing enthusiasts and newcomers to the world of steeplechase.

Conclusion: Red Rum's unique story and origins set the stage for an extraordinary career that defied expectations and captivated a nation. In the chapters that follow, we will delve deeper into his historic Grand National victories and the impact of this remarkable bay horse with a heart of a champion. Red Rum's legacy is a testament to the enduring magic of steeplechase racing and the enduring fascination with the shadows of silver that continue to illuminate the sport.

The Remarkable Grand National Wins

Red Rum's legacy in the world of horse racing is indelibly linked to his unprecedented successes in the Grand National, one of the most grueling and revered steeplechase races on the planet. In this chapter, we delve into the remarkable Grand National wins of Red Rum, tracing the paths to victory that established him as a true Aintree legend and one of the greatest steeplechasers in history.

The Aintree Challenge: Aintree Racecourse in Liverpool, England, is synonymous with the Grand National, a race that pushes horses and jockeys to their limits. Its demanding course, characterized by towering fences and a grueling distance, is considered one of the ultimate tests of endurance and jumping ability. Red Rum's victories in this iconic event are the stuff of legend.

First Victory in 1973: In 1973, Red Rum achieved his first Grand National victory. Guided by jockey Brian Fletcher, he displayed a remarkable combination of courage and stamina, surging ahead to claim the title. It was an electrifying moment that marked the beginning of an extraordinary era.

Repeat Triumph in 1974: Red Rum's victory in 1973 was no fluke. The following year, he returned to Aintree with an ardent fan following. His second consecutive win in the

Grand National, under jockey Brian Fletcher once again, catapulted him to superstardom. His back-to-back victories were a testament to his unmatched prowess on the Aintree course.

Runner-Up in 1975: In 1975, Red Rum demonstrated his enduring spirit by finishing in second place, narrowly missing out on a historic hat-trick of victories. His remarkable performance as a 12-year-old horse was celebrated as a triumph in its own right, and he remained the beloved people's horse.

Return to Glory in 1977: After a brief retirement and a spell as a public figurehead for the sport, Red Rum made a stunning return to Aintree in 1977. At the age of 12, he defied the odds to secure his third Grand National win, an achievement that remains unmatched in the history of the race. Ridden by jockey Tommy Stack, his victory was a fairytale ending to an extraordinary career.

Enduring Legacy: Red Rum's Grand National wins were not merely athletic achievements; they were moments that transcended the sport of horse racing. His tenacity, his affinity for the Aintree course, and his ability to capture the public's imagination turned him into a national hero. His wins symbolized the triumph of the underdog, resonating with a nation that celebrated his victories as their own.

The People's Horse: Red Rum's appeal extended beyond the racing world. He was a horse that belonged to the people, and his Grand National victories were celebrated with a fervor that rivaled the fervent cheering at Aintree. His legacy endures as a reminder of the magical and unifying power of sports.

The Aintree Legend: Red Rum's name became synonymous with the Grand National, and his spirit lives on in the very heart of the Aintree course. The iconic steeplechase race remains a testament to his unparalleled achievements, and each year, his memory is invoked as new horses and jockeys tackle the Aintree challenge.

Conclusion: Red Rum's remarkable Grand National wins not only established him as a legend of steeplechase racing but also left an indelible mark on the history of the sport. His unique story and triumphant victories at Aintree continue to inspire generations of racing enthusiasts, reminding us of the enduring allure and magic of the Grand National and the shadows of silver that illuminate the world of horse racing.

The Enduring Popularity of a Horse with a "Grey" Reputation

Red Rum, a bay horse whose coat appeared grey due to fading with age, transcended the boundaries of traditional horse racing fame. His remarkable story, coupled with his unique appearance, contributed to the enduring popularity of a horse with a "grey" reputation. In this chapter, we delve into the reasons behind Red Rum's enduring appeal and the significant impact he had on both racing enthusiasts and the wider public.

The Silver Mirage: Red Rum's bay coat, which lightened with age, gave him the appearance of a grey horse. This distinctive feature not only set him apart but also added to his mystique. His unique coat color became one of the defining characteristics of his legacy.

Underdog Status: In the world of horse racing, grey horses are often viewed as underdogs. The tradition of "grey horses" symbolizing less-favored competitors provided an additional layer of charm to Red Rum's story. His ability to overcome the odds and secure unprecedented Grand National victories endeared him to fans who saw him as an embodiment of resilience and the triumph of the underdog.

The People's Horse: Red Rum's connection with the public was profound. He was not just a horse for seasoned racing enthusiasts but a figure who captured the imagination of people from all walks of life. His victories in the Grand National were celebrated as victories for the ordinary person, and he became "the people's horse."

Storytelling and Media: The media played a significant role in shaping Red Rum's image. His unique appearance and dramatic Grand National wins were ripe material for storytelling. Books, films, and documentaries further elevated his status, making him an iconic figure in British popular culture.

National Hero: Red Rum's fame extended beyond the racetrack. He became a symbol of national pride, a source of hope and inspiration during challenging times. His popularity resonated with a nation that had endured economic hardships and celebrated his victories as their own.

Marketing and Merchandising: Red Rum's image appeared on a wide range of products, from posters and clothing to memorabilia. His name and likeness were used to market everything from beer to betting companies, cementing his status as a commercial icon.

Public Appearances: Even in retirement, Red Rum remained in the public eye. He made appearances at racetracks and events, connecting with fans and further strengthening his status as a beloved figure. His public engagements served to preserve his legacy and keep his story alive.

Educational Impact: Red Rum's story is not just about racing; it's also about the power of perseverance, the bond between horse and rider, and the magic of the Grand National. His story continues to be used in educational contexts to teach lessons about determination and the history of the sport.

Legacy in the Racing World: Red Rum's enduring popularity transcended generations, and his name remains synonymous with the Grand National. His legacy continues to influence the world of steeplechase racing, inspiring jockeys and horses to strive for greatness on the Aintree course.

Conclusion: Red Rum's unique appearance, combined with his remarkable accomplishments, transformed him into a cultural and sporting phenomenon. His "grey" reputation and enduring popularity serve as a testament to the enduring fascination with the world of horse racing and the shadows of silver that continue to illuminate the sport. In the chapters that follow, we will explore more facets of Red Rum's incredible journey and his lasting impact on the racing world.

Red Rum's Impact on the Grand National

Red Rum's name is inextricably linked with the Grand National, a race that defined his career and solidified his status as an icon in the world of horse racing. In this chapter, we delve into the profound impact that Red Rum had on the Grand National, a race he not only conquered but transformed, leaving an indelible mark on the history and legacy of this prestigious steeplechase event.

Aintree's Favorite Son: Aintree Racecourse, the home of the Grand National, holds a special place in the hearts of racing enthusiasts. Red Rum's enduring connection with Aintree transformed him into one of the most beloved figures in the history of the race. He became Aintree's favorite son, and the course became his legendary playground.

Reviving Interest: In the 1970s, the Grand National faced challenges to its prestige and popularity. The course had become perilous, and tragedies had occurred, leading to calls for reform. Red Rum's victories in 1973 and 1974 injected new life into the race. His remarkable successes helped reignite interest and enthusiasm for the Grand National.

Safety and Course Improvements: Red Rum's victories prompted a reevaluation of the Aintree course. Safety measures were introduced, including modifications to the fences and ground conditions, to reduce the risk to both horses and jockeys. His impact went beyond winning races; it contributed to a safer and more regulated Grand National.

The Triple Crown: Red Rum's unprecedented feat of winning three Grand Nationals (in 1973, 1974, and 1977) remains a milestone in the history of the race. His record-breaking achievement elevated the Grand National to new heights, making it a must-watch event for racing fans around the world.

A National Hero: Red Rum's victories in the Grand National transcended horse racing. He became a symbol of national pride, a unifying figure during a time of economic hardship in Britain. The nation rallied around him, celebrating his triumphs as symbols of hope and resilience.

Renewed Public Interest: The Grand National, once at risk of losing its appeal, saw a surge in public interest and television viewership during Red Rum's era. His victories brought the race to a wider audience, and it became an annual spectacle watched by millions.

Educational Tool: Red Rum's story continues to be used in educational contexts to teach about the history and significance of the Grand National. His legacy serves as a powerful educational tool for students of horse racing and sports history.

Commercial and Marketing Impact: Red Rum's association with the Grand National also had a significant commercial impact. His name and likeness were used for various promotions, cementing his status as a commercial icon and contributing to the race's popularity.

Legacy for Future Generations: Red Rum's legacy lives on, inspiring future generations of jockeys, trainers, and horses. His extraordinary performances in the Grand National continue to serve as a source of motivation and aspiration for those who aim to make their mark on the Aintree course.

Conclusion: Red Rum's impact on the Grand National was transformative, rejuvenating the race, making it safer, and turning it into a global spectacle. His enduring influence ensures that the Grand National remains not just a race but a celebration of horse racing's history and the enduring allure of the shadows of silver that continue to illuminate the world of the sport.

Chapter 3: Spectacular Bid (United States, 1976-1981), Grey

Spectacular Bid's Early Career and Promise

Spectacular Bid, the grey thoroughbred born in 1976, embarked on a journey that would see him become one of the most promising and electrifying racehorses in American horse racing history. In this chapter, we explore the early career of Spectacular Bid, his early races, and the promise he displayed as he burst onto the racing scene.

A Star is Born: Spectacular Bid's journey began on February 17, 1976, when he was foaled in Kentucky. Bred by Grover G. "Buddy" Delp, he was sired by Bold Bidder and foaled by Spectacular, and from his early days, he displayed an extraordinary blend of genetics that would set him apart.

Early Training and Development: Spectacular Bid's early training under the guidance of trainer Bud Delp and jockey Ronnie Franklin was a crucial phase in his development. The horse showcased a natural aptitude for racing, impressing his handlers with his speed, agility, and determination.

Two-Year-Old Season: Spectacular Bid made his racing debut as a two-year-old, and it didn't take long for him to announce his presence. His early victories and performances demonstrated his potential as a top-class racehorse. The racing world began to take notice of the striking grey colt.

Unbeaten Streak: Spectacular Bid's two-year-old season was marked by an unbeaten streak, a testament to his exceptional talent. He not only won races but did so convincingly, establishing himself as one of the most promising young horses in the United States.

The Eclipse Award: Spectacular Bid's extraordinary performances in his debut season earned him the prestigious Eclipse Award for Champion Two-Year-Old Male Horse. This recognition was a clear sign that he was destined for greatness in the world of American horse racing.

Three-Year-Old Season: As Spectacular Bid transitioned into his three-year-old season, the anticipation and expectations surrounding him continued to grow. His performances in prep races and early contests served as a preview of the remarkable year that lay ahead.

Kentucky Derby: The Kentucky Derby, the first leg of the Triple Crown, was the most eagerly anticipated race of Spectacular Bid's career. His victory in the Derby not only confirmed his status as a rising star but also placed him firmly on the path to racing immortality.

The Preakness Stakes: Following his Kentucky Derby triumph, Spectacular Bid's quest for the Triple Crown led him to the Preakness Stakes. The race was marked by controversy and an unexpected defeat, which would become a defining moment in his career.

Promise and Potential: Despite the Preakness setback, Spectacular Bid's early career was brimming with promise and potential. His speed, versatility, and charisma made him a horse to watch, and the racing world eagerly awaited his future performances.

Conclusion: Spectacular Bid's early career was marked by the promise of a horse destined for greatness. His victories and performances as a two-year-old and three-year-old set the stage for an extraordinary journey in American horse racing. In the chapters that follow, we will continue to explore the highs and lows of his career, his enduring legacy, and the indomitable spirit that defined him.

The 1979 Kentucky Derby and Preakness Stakes Wins

Spectacular Bid's journey to racing greatness reached a pivotal moment in 1979 when he embarked on the Kentucky Derby and Preakness Stakes, the first two legs of the Triple Crown. In this chapter, we delve into the thrilling victories of Spectacular Bid in the 1979 Kentucky Derby and Preakness Stakes, races that showcased his exceptional talent and brought him one step closer to horse racing immortality.

The Kentucky Derby: The Run for the Roses: The Kentucky Derby, often referred to as the "Run for the Roses," is one of the most prestigious and iconic races in American horse racing. In 1979, all eyes were on Spectacular Bid as he entered the starting gate at Churchill Downs, Kentucky.

High Expectations: Spectacular Bid was the clear favorite in the Kentucky Derby, thanks to his unbeaten streak and remarkable performances as a three-year-old. The racing world had high expectations for the grey colt, but the pressure of the Triple Crown weighed heavily.

Victory in Style: Spectacular Bid's victory in the 1979 Kentucky Derby was nothing short of spectacular. He demonstrated his incredible speed and versatility, surging ahead in the final furlongs and crossing the finish line with a comfortable lead. The win solidified his status as a Triple Crown contender and a horse of exceptional ability.

Controversy and the 'Safety Pin' Incident: The Kentucky Derby victory was, however, marred by a controversial incident known as the "Safety Pin" incident. A stray safety pin in Spectacular Bid's stall reportedly caused a minor injury to his hoof. This incident fueled concerns about his well-being as he headed to the Preakness Stakes.

The Preakness Stakes: The Second Leg: Following his triumphant Kentucky Derby victory, Spectacular Bid's next challenge was the Preakness Stakes, the second leg of the Triple Crown. The race took place at Pimlico Race Course in Baltimore, Maryland.

Preakness Dominance: Spectacular Bid's performance in the Preakness Stakes was nothing short of dominant. He put to rest any doubts about his condition and readiness, winning the race by several lengths. His victory not only showcased his speed and stamina but also reinforced his status as the horse to beat in the Triple Crown quest.

A Flawless Campaign: Spectacular Bid's wins in the Kentucky Derby and Preakness Stakes were part of a near-flawless campaign in 1979. He had captured the imagination of the racing world, and the prospect of a Triple Crown victory seemed within reach.

The Triple Crown Quest: With victories in the first two legs, Spectacular Bid stood on the precipice of Triple Crown glory. The anticipation and excitement among racing fans were palpable as he headed to the Belmont Stakes, the final and most challenging leg of the Triple Crown.

Conclusion: Spectacular Bid's wins in the 1979 Kentucky Derby and Preakness Stakes were pivotal moments in his career. These races demonstrated his exceptional talent and placed him on the brink of Triple Crown history. In the chapters that follow, we will explore the challenges and triumphs that awaited Spectacular Bid in his quest for horse racing immortality.

The Controversy and Aftermath of the Belmont Stakes

The Belmont Stakes of 1979 marked a turning point in the career of Spectacular Bid and is remembered as one of the most controversial and dramatic moments in the history of American horse racing. In this chapter, we delve into the events, controversies, and the aftermath of the Belmont Stakes that had a profound impact on the legacy of the grey colt, Spectacular Bid.

The Triple Crown Elusive: Spectacular Bid entered the Belmont Stakes as the overwhelming favorite, with the Triple Crown within his grasp. Victory in this race would secure his place in the annals of horse racing history as one of the few horses to achieve the illustrious Triple Crown.

The Early Stages: In the early stages of the Belmont Stakes, Spectacular Bid appeared poised for another victory. He took the lead and was seemingly in control of the race. The crowd at Belmont Park was filled with anticipation.

The Controversial Move: However, as the race progressed, a fateful move by jockey Ronnie Franklin altered the course of the race. Franklin, riding Spectacular Bid, inexplicably urged the horse to make an early and ill-timed move, putting him under unnecessary strain.

The Loss: Spectacular Bid's early exertion in the race took its toll, and he faltered in the final stretch. He finished third in the Belmont Stakes, missing out on the Triple Crown. The loss was a heartbreaking moment for racing fans and cast a shadow of controversy on the race.

The Aftermath: The aftermath of the Belmont Stakes was marked by speculation, scrutiny, and debates. Questions were raised about Ronnie Franklin's strategy and whether the move had cost Spectacular Bid the Triple Crown. The racing world was left to ponder what might have been.

The Role of the Media: The media played a significant role in dissecting the events of the Belmont Stakes. Analysts, journalists, and commentators offered their perspectives on what had transpired, contributing to the ongoing controversy and discussion.

Impact on Spectacular Bid's Legacy: The Belmont Stakes loss had a lasting impact on Spectacular Bid's legacy. While he had enjoyed remarkable success as a racehorse, the shadow of the Triple Crown defeat would always be part of his story. The loss added complexity to his legacy, marking a moment of vulnerability in an otherwise illustrious career.

Legacy Beyond the Triple Crown: Spectacular Bid's legacy transcended the disappointment of the Belmont Stakes. He continued to race successfully, earning honors and setting records. His impact on American horse racing extended well beyond the elusive Triple Crown.

Retirement and Influence: Spectacular Bid's racing career eventually came to a close, but his influence endured. He became a prominent stallion, siring a new generation of racehorses, many of which carried on his legacy on the racetrack.

Conclusion: The controversy and aftermath of the Belmont Stakes were defining moments in Spectacular Bid's career. They added layers of complexity to his story and solidified his place in the annals of American horse racing. In the chapters that follow, we will explore the latter stages of his career and the lasting impact of this remarkable grey colt.

The Enduring Appeal of a Horse Destined for Greatness

Spectacular Bid's journey in the world of horse racing was one marked by exceptional talent, record-breaking performances, and a unique aura of greatness. In this chapter, we explore the enduring appeal of Spectacular Bid, a horse whose destiny was intertwined with the pursuit of greatness, leaving an indelible mark on the hearts of racing enthusiasts and the sport as a whole.

The Grey Phenomenon: Spectacular Bid's striking grey coat, paired with his impressive physical attributes and on-track performances, made him an unmistakable figure on the racetrack. His distinctive appearance added to his allure, capturing the imagination of fans.

Early Successes and Promise: From his early races as a two-year-old to his standout performances in the Kentucky Derby and Preakness Stakes, Spectacular Bid showcased promise and potential that set him apart from his contemporaries. Racing enthusiasts recognized that they were witnessing the emergence of a once-in-a-generation talent.

Triple Crown Aspirations: Spectacular Bid's pursuit of the Triple Crown ignited the hopes and dreams of racing fans. The quest for the elusive Triple Crown, an accomplishment achieved by only a select few, added an element of historic significance to his career.

Heartbreak at the Belmont Stakes: The dramatic events of the Belmont Stakes, where Spectacular Bid narrowly missed securing the Triple Crown, left a lasting impact on his legacy. The loss was a moment of vulnerability for a horse that had appeared invincible, but it also revealed his resilience in the face of adversity.

Record-Breaking Performances: Spectacular Bid's career was defined by record-breaking performances. He set new standards in various races, including the Strub Stakes, the San Fernando Stakes, and the Marlboro Cup. His achievements further solidified his status as a racing legend.

Endurance and Versatility: Spectacular Bid's ability to perform at various distances and on different surfaces showcased his versatility. He demonstrated remarkable endurance and adaptability, making him a true all-around racehorse.

The Public's Horse: Spectacular Bid's appeal extended beyond the racing community. He became "the public's horse," a figure who transcended the boundaries of the sport. His victories were celebrated as collective triumphs, and his story served as a source of inspiration and pride.

Media Spotlight: The media played a pivotal role in shaping Spectacular Bid's image and disseminating his story. Journalists, photographers, and broadcasters helped convey the excitement and drama of his career to a wide audience.

Commercial and Marketing Icon: Spectacular Bid's name and likeness were used in various marketing and promotional campaigns. His image adorned posters, merchandise, and advertisements, cementing his status as a commercial icon.

Influence Beyond the Track: Spectacular Bid's impact extended beyond his racing career. As a stallion, he left a legacy, siring a new generation of racehorses that carried forward his bloodline and his spirit on the racetrack.

Conclusion: Spectacular Bid's enduring appeal is a testament to the enduring magic of horse racing. His striking grey coat, remarkable performances, and unyielding spirit made him a figure of inspiration and fascination. In the chapters that follow, we will continue to explore the later stages of his career and the legacy he left on the world of horse racing.

Chapter 4: Kincsem ((Hungary, 1874-1887), Grey
The Story of the Undefeated Hungarian Legend

Kincsem, the remarkable grey mare born in 1874, holds a special place in the annals of horse racing history as one of the most legendary and undefeated racehorses of all time. In this chapter, we embark on a journey into the story of Kincsem, the Hungarian sensation who etched her name in the record books and captured the hearts of racing enthusiasts across the globe.

Birth of a Legend: Kincsem was foaled in Hungary in 1874, and from the moment of her birth, it was evident that she was a horse of exceptional qualities. Her breeding, lineage, and physical attributes set the stage for a remarkable racing career.

The Hungarian Racing Scene: The late 19th century marked the height of horse racing in Hungary, and Kincsem emerged as a symbol of national pride. Racing was a popular sport in the country, and Kincsem's success resonated with a fervent racing audience.

Early Races and Domination: Kincsem's racing career began with a series of dominant performances. Her early races showcased her exceptional speed and agility, and it became evident that she was a force to be reckoned with on the track.

Unbeaten Streak: Kincsem's defining feature was her unbeaten streak. Race after race, she left her competitors in her wake, emerging victorious with remarkable consistency. Her unbeaten run became the stuff of legend.

International Acclaim: Kincsem's reputation extended beyond Hungary. Her international acclaim grew as she competed and triumphed in races across Europe. Her victories in prestigious events added to her aura of invincibility.

The Jockey and Trainer Connection: The partnership between Kincsem and her jockey, Hungarian riding legend Mihály Farcas, was central to her success. Farcas's skill and understanding of the mare's abilities played a pivotal role in maintaining her unbeaten streak.

The Challenges and Rivalries: While Kincsem was largely dominant, she did face challenges and rivals along the way. Her ability to overcome competitors and adversities further cemented her status as a legendary racehorse.

Retirement and Legacy: Kincsem's racing career eventually came to a close, but her legacy endured. She retired as an undefeated racehorse, a feat rarely achieved in the history of the sport. Her legacy extended to future generations of racehorses and racing enthusiasts.

Impact on Hungarian Identity: Kincsem's victories and her status as a national hero had a profound impact on Hungarian identity and culture. She became a symbol of pride, resilience, and the nation's racing heritage.

Recognition and Tributes: Kincsem's achievements did not go unnoticed. She received recognition and accolades both in her time and posthumously, including monuments, statues, and various tributes dedicated to her memory.

Conclusion: The story of Kincsem, the undefeated Hungarian legend, is one of enduring fascination and inspiration. Her remarkable racing career and unbeaten streak set her apart as an icon in the world of horse racing. In the chapters that follow, we will continue to explore her global recognition, her legacy in Hungary, and the enduring impact of this extraordinary grey mare.

Kincsem's Global Recognition and Unmatched Record

Kincsem, the remarkable grey mare born in Hungary in 1874, achieved a level of global recognition that few racehorses in history can match. Her unbeaten record, combined with her breathtaking performances, made her an international sensation. In this chapter, we explore Kincsem's global recognition and her unmatched record, highlighting the impact she had on the world of horse racing and the hearts of racing enthusiasts across the globe.

A Horse of International Acclaim: Kincsem's name transcended borders and became synonymous with excellence in horse racing. Her performances in Europe and beyond drew attention from racing enthusiasts, royalty, and the media. Her international acclaim set her apart as a true global icon.

Racing Across Europe: Kincsem's journey took her to various European countries, where she competed in prestigious races and faced top-class competition. Her victories in Germany, Austria, France, and England solidified her reputation as a horse of extraordinary talent.

Triumphs in Prestigious Races: Kincsem's resume was adorned with victories in some of the most renowned races in Europe. The likes of the Goodwood Cup in England, the

Prix de l'Arc de Triomphe in France, and the Grosser Preis von Baden in Germany were among her conquests.

Unbeaten Streak and Record-Breaking Wins: One of the most remarkable aspects of Kincsem's career was her unbeaten streak. Race after race, she crossed the finish line first, an achievement that remains unmatched in the history of horse racing. Her record-breaking wins captured the imaginations of fans worldwide.

Recognition by European Royalty: Kincsem's success did not go unnoticed by European royalty. Her wins earned her the admiration and patronage of kings, queens, and nobility. Her presence at races became a regal spectacle, further elevating her status.

The Impact on European Horse Racing: Kincsem's dominance in European racing had a profound impact on the sport. She raised the bar for competition and set a standard of excellence that future racehorses would aspire to. Her legacy in European horse racing is enduring.

The Global Media Sensation: Kincsem's performances were closely followed by the media, and her story was reported in newspapers, journals, and periodicals across the world. She became a media sensation, captivating audiences far beyond the racetracks.

Her Impact on Hungary: Kincsem's success resonated deeply with the people of Hungary. She became a symbol of national pride and identity, reinforcing the country's connection to horse racing. Her legacy in Hungary is celebrated to this day.

Tributes and Statues: Kincsem's legacy lives on through numerous tributes and statues dedicated to her memory. Her image and achievements continue to be honored, serving as a source of inspiration for future generations.

Conclusion: Kincsem's global recognition and unmatched record place her in the pantheon of the world's greatest racehorses. Her extraordinary career elevated her to legendary status, and her impact on the world of horse racing endures as a source of inspiration and fascination. In the chapters that follow, we will continue to explore her influence and the lasting legacy she left on the racing world.

Kincsem's Legacy in Hungary and the Racing World

Kincsem, the extraordinary grey mare born in Hungary in 1874, not only achieved international acclaim with her unbeaten record and record-breaking wins but also left an enduring legacy in her home country and the broader world of horse racing. In this chapter, we delve into Kincsem's legacy in Hungary and the racing world, exploring how her remarkable career and her indomitable spirit continue to resonate with racing enthusiasts and professionals to this day.

Hungary's National Treasure: Kincsem's legacy in Hungary is nothing short of iconic. She is considered a national treasure, and her name is synonymous with excellence in horse racing. Her impact on Hungarian identity and culture remains deeply rooted.

Inspiration for Aspiring Jockeys and Trainers: Kincsem's success inspired generations of Hungarian jockeys and trainers. Her story became a symbol of aspiration, encouraging young riders to pursue their dreams in the world of horse racing.

Honoring Her Memory: Kincsem's legacy is celebrated through various tributes and memorials across Hungary. Statues, plaques, and dedicated spaces serve as reminders of her remarkable career and the pride she brought to the nation.

Contribution to Hungarian Racing: Kincsem's triumphs on the international stage invigorated the Hungarian racing scene. Her success encouraged investment in the sport and the breeding of top-class racehorses, ensuring the continued growth and development of horse racing in Hungary.

Legacy in Training and Breeding: Kincsem's career left an indelible mark on training techniques and breeding practices in Hungary. Her excellence set new standards and influenced the way horses were trained and bred for generations to come.

The Impact on Hungarian Culture: Kincsem's influence extended beyond horse racing. Her legacy is woven into the fabric of Hungarian culture, with her name and achievements referenced in literature, art, and folklore.

National Pride and Resilience: Kincsem's unbeaten streak became a symbol of Hungarian resilience and determination. She embodied the spirit of never giving up and striving for greatness, qualities that resonate with the nation's history and character.

The Global Racing Community: Beyond Hungary, Kincsem's legacy had a profound impact on the global racing community. Her achievements demonstrated that exceptional racehorses could emerge from unexpected places and take on the world's best.

Influence on Modern Racing: Kincsem's racing career set benchmarks for excellence that continue to inspire modern racehorses, jockeys, and trainers. Her story serves as a reminder of what can be achieved in the world of horse racing.

Continued Fascination: Even more than a century after her racing career, Kincsem's story continues to fascinate racing enthusiasts. Books, documentaries, and retrospectives keep her legend alive, and her name remains synonymous with the enduring appeal of horse racing.

Conclusion: Kincsem's legacy in Hungary and the racing world is a testament to the enduring power of exceptional racehorses to inspire and captivate the hearts of a nation and the racing community. Her name lives on as a symbol of excellence, national pride, and the timeless allure of the sport. In the chapters that follow, we will explore the broader impact of her legend and the lasting influence she had on the world of horse racing.

The Extraordinary Journey of a White-Coated Heroine

Kincsem, the exceptional grey mare born in Hungary in 1874, embarked on an extraordinary journey that saw her become one of the most celebrated and undefeated racehorses in history. Her remarkable career and indomitable spirit continue to inspire racing enthusiasts and professionals alike. In this chapter, we delve into the extraordinary journey of Kincsem, a white-coated heroine whose impact on the world of horse racing is nothing short of legendary.

Early Life and Beginnings: Kincsem's journey began in the Hungarian countryside, where she was foaled and raised. Her early life and upbringing laid the foundation for her future success on the racetrack.

The Unbeaten Streak: Kincsem's defining feature was her unbeaten streak. Race after race, she crossed the finish line first, an achievement that remains unmatched in the history of horse racing. We explore the races that contributed to this remarkable record.

International Success: Kincsem's racing career took her to various European countries, where she competed in prestigious races and emerged victorious. Her international acclaim grew as she triumphed in events such as the

Goodwood Cup, the Prix de l'Arc de Triomphe, and the Grosser Preis von Baden.

Rivalries and Challenges: While Kincsem enjoyed dominance, she did face challenges and formidable rivals. We explore the moments when she was pushed to her limits and how she responded with resilience and determination.

Recognition by European Royalty: Kincsem's success did not go unnoticed by European royalty. Her wins earned her the admiration and patronage of kings, queens, and nobility. Her presence at races became a regal spectacle, further elevating her status.

The Impact on European Racing: Kincsem's dominance in European racing had a profound impact on the sport. She raised the bar for competition and set a standard of excellence that future racehorses would aspire to. Her legacy in European horse racing is enduring.

Recognition and Tributes: Kincsem's achievements did not go unnoticed. She received recognition and accolades both in her time and posthumously, including monuments, statues, and various tributes dedicated to her memory.

Influence on Modern Racing: Kincsem's racing career set benchmarks for excellence that continue to inspire modern racehorses, jockeys, and trainers. Her story serves as a reminder of what can be achieved in the world of horse racing.

Continued Fascination: Even more than a century after her racing career, Kincsem's story continues to fascinate racing enthusiasts. Books, documentaries, and retrospectives keep her legend alive, and her name remains synonymous with the enduring appeal of horse racing.

Conclusion: Kincsem's journey is a testament to the extraordinary potential of racehorses to captivate hearts and inspire generations. Her remarkable career and indomitable spirit are etched into the annals of horse racing history, where she stands as a symbol of excellence and the enduring allure of the sport. In the chapters that follow, we will continue to explore the broader impact of her legend and the lasting influence she had on the world of horse racing.

Chapter 5: Shadows in the Pantheon
Exploring the Presence and Significance of White and Grey-Coated Horses in Racing History

White and grey-coated horses have long held a unique and captivating place in the history of horse racing. These striking horses, known as "Shadows of Silver," have captured the imagination of racing enthusiasts and have left an indelible mark on the sport. In this chapter, we delve into the presence and significance of white and grey-coated horses in racing history, uncovering the mystique and allure that has surrounded these equine stars for generations.

The Elegance of the Grey Coat: Grey-coated horses, often described as "dappled grays," possess a distinct and elegant appearance. We explore the fascination and admiration that have surrounded grey horses in racing, with a focus on their aesthetic appeal.

The Rarity of True White: True white-coated horses are rare in the equine world, making their presence in racing all the more remarkable. We examine the genetics behind white-coated horses and the intrigue they generate among racing enthusiasts.

Historical White and Grey Champions: Throughout racing history, several white and grey-coated horses have achieved legendary status. We discuss notable champions like Kincsem, The Tetrarch, and Desert Orchid, highlighting their unique contributions to the sport.

The Symbolism of Grey and White: In various cultures and traditions, white and grey horses hold symbolic significance. We explore the symbolism associated with these coat colors and how it has influenced their portrayal in folklore and myth.

Advantages and Challenges: Grey and white-coated horses often face distinct challenges, including increased susceptibility to skin conditions and sunburn. However, their coats also provide certain advantages, such as improved heat reflection.

The Racing Records: We delve into the records and achievements of white and grey-coated horses throughout history, emphasizing their remarkable performances on the racetrack. These records serve as a testament to their exceptional abilities.

Mystique and Allure: The mystique surrounding white and grey-coated horses is palpable. We explore the aura of uniqueness and intrigue that these horses bring to the racing world, captivating fans and industry professionals.

The Modern Era: While the prevalence of white-coated horses has decreased in modern racing, grey-coated horses continue to make their mark. We discuss contemporary grey champions and their influence on the sport.

Contemporary Challenges: In the modern era, white and grey-coated horses face new challenges, including issues related to health and care. We discuss how the racing industry addresses these challenges and ensures the well-being of these unique horses.

Conclusion: The presence and significance of white and grey-coated horses in racing history are a testament to the enduring fascination and allure of the sport. These horses, with their distinctive coats, have not only left an indelible mark on the racetrack but have also captured the hearts of racing enthusiasts worldwide. In the chapters that follow, we will explore the bonds between these extraordinary horses and their skilled jockeys, the records they shattered, and the lasting impact they've had on the world of horse racing.

The Unique Challenges and Advantages of These Coat Colors

White and grey-coated horses, known as "Shadows of Silver," bring a distinct charm to the world of horse racing. Their striking appearance and unique coat colors make them stand out on the racetrack. However, these coat colors come with their own set of challenges and advantages that set them apart from their bay, chestnut, and black counterparts. In this chapter, we explore the unique challenges and advantages that white and grey-coated horses face in the world of horse racing.

The Allure of the Grey Coat: Grey-coated horses often have a dappled, silvery appearance that many find visually appealing. Their aesthetic allure can capture the hearts of racing enthusiasts and make them a memorable presence on the track.

Rarity and Mystique: White-coated horses, in particular, are quite rare in the equine world. Their scarcity adds to their mystique and intrigue, making them unique and highly sought-after by collectors and breeders.

Sun Sensitivity: White-coated and grey-coated horses are more susceptible to sunburn and skin conditions due to their lack of pigmentation. This sensitivity requires extra care, including the use of sunscreen and protective clothing, especially in sunny climates.

Coat Changes with Age: Grey-coated horses often undergo coat changes as they age, which can affect their appearance and create variations in the shade of grey. These changes add an element of surprise to their careers, as they may look quite different in their later years.

The Challenge of Staying Clean: Grey-coated horses can be particularly challenging to keep clean, especially in muddy or wet conditions. Trainers and grooms often face the task of keeping their horses' coats looking pristine, which can be an ongoing effort.

Advantages in Warm Weather: White-coated horses have the advantage of reflecting sunlight, which can help keep them cooler in warm weather. This can be advantageous for performance, as overheating can impact a horse's stamina.

Unique Aesthetic on the Track: Grey and white-coated horses create a unique and captivating visual spectacle on the racetrack. Their striking appearance can add an element of excitement and elegance to racing events.

Heritage and Tradition: In some cultures and traditions, grey-coated horses are considered especially auspicious or symbolic. Their presence in certain events may carry cultural significance and heritage.

The Challenge of Maintaining Appearance: White and grey-coated horses require meticulous grooming and care to maintain their appearance. This can be a labor-intensive process, but the results are often worth the effort.

The Bond Between Horse and Handler: The extra care and attention required for white and grey-coated horses can foster a strong bond between the horse and its handler or groom. The trust and rapport between them are vital for the horse's well-being.

Conclusion: The unique challenges and advantages of white and grey-coated horses add depth to the world of horse racing. While these horses may require extra care, their striking appearance and distinctive qualities make them an integral part of the sport's rich tapestry. In the chapters that follow, we will continue to explore the shared characteristics of these extraordinary horses, the skilled jockeys who rode them to victory, and the records they shattered on the racetrack.

The Shared Characteristics of These Legendary Horses

White and grey-coated horses, often referred to as "Shadows of Silver," have left an indelible mark on the world of horse racing. Despite their unique coat colors, these equine champions share certain characteristics that have contributed to their legendary status. In this chapter, we explore the shared traits and qualities that define these extraordinary horses, transcending the boundaries of color and breed to create a collective legacy in the world of racing.

Exceptional Resilience: One common trait among these legendary horses is exceptional resilience. They have shown the ability to overcome challenges, whether on the racetrack or in their physical characteristics. This resilience has made them stand out as true champions.

Unyielding Spirit: White and grey-coated horses often exhibit an unyielding spirit and determination. Their innate drive to succeed, combined with their physical prowess, has propelled them to the pinnacle of racing success.

Natural Athleticism: These horses possess a natural athleticism that goes beyond their unique coat colors. Their agility, speed, and strength are qualities that all racing enthusiasts and professionals recognize and admire.

Versatility: Many white and grey-coated horses have demonstrated versatility in their racing careers. They have excelled in various race distances and on different surfaces, showcasing their adaptability and all-around abilities.

Innate Showmanship: There's a certain showmanship that often accompanies these horses. Their presence on the racetrack is commanding, and they seem to revel in the attention and the spotlight.

Consistency in Performance: One of the defining characteristics of these legendary horses is their consistency in performance. Whether through an unbeaten streak or a string of remarkable victories, they have proven themselves as reliable competitors.

Endurance and Stamina: Endurance and stamina are qualities shared by these equine stars. They've demonstrated the ability to maintain their speed and energy over long distances, a vital trait for success in horse racing.

Mental Toughness: Mental toughness is a common trait among these horses. They've shown the ability to remain focused and determined even in the face of adversity or competition.

Fondness for Challenges: Many white and grey-coated horses seem to thrive on challenges. Whether facing fierce rivals or tackling new racecourses, they've risen to the occasion, often producing their best performances when pushed to their limits.

Connection with Their Jockeys: The bond between these horses and their jockeys is often strong and special. The trust and understanding between horse and rider have played a pivotal role in their success on the racetrack.

Enduring Legacy: Perhaps the most significant shared characteristic among these horses is the enduring legacy they've left in the world of horse racing. Their stories continue to inspire and fascinate generations of racing enthusiasts and professionals.

Conclusion: The shared characteristics of these legendary white and grey-coated horses transcend their physical appearances. Their resilience, spirit, athleticism, and the qualities that have made them exceptional champions have left an indelible mark on the world of horse racing. In the chapters that follow, we will continue to explore the skilled jockeys who rode these remarkable horses to victory, the records they shattered, and the lasting impact they've had on the racing world.

Chapter 6: The Jockeys Behind the Legends
The Skilled Jockeys Who Rode These Legendary Horses to Victory

Behind every great racehorse, there is often a skilled and dedicated jockey who plays a pivotal role in their success. In this chapter, we shift our focus from the horses themselves to the talented individuals who rode these legendary white and grey-coated champions to victory. These jockeys, with their unique skills, unshakable bonds with their equine partners, and unwavering determination, are an integral part of the stories that make horse racing so captivating.

The Art of Race Riding: Race riding is an art, and skilled jockeys are the masters. We delve into the techniques and strategies that jockeys employ to guide their horses to triumph, emphasizing the importance of timing, balance, and communication.

The Bond Between Horse and Rider: The connection between a jockey and their mount is essential for success on the racetrack. We explore the unique relationships that developed between these jockeys and their white and grey-coated champions, highlighting the trust and understanding that formed the foundation of their partnerships.

Understanding Individual Horses: Each horse is unique, and jockeys must understand their horses' strengths, weaknesses, and idiosyncrasies. We discuss how these jockeys developed an intimate knowledge of their equine partners, enabling them to bring out the best in their mounts.

Race Strategy and Tactics: Race tactics are crucial for success in horse racing. We analyze the strategic decisions made by jockeys, including when to make a move, how to position their horses, and when to push for that final burst of speed.

Balancing Act: Maintaining balance on a galloping horse is no small feat. We explore the physical demands placed on jockeys and their ability to maintain equilibrium while urging their mounts to the finish line.

Challenges and Risks: Jockeys face numerous challenges and risks in the pursuit of victory. We discuss the dangers they encounter, from injury to the constant pressure to maintain a low body weight.

Jockeys Behind the Legends: We spotlight the individual jockeys who rode these legendary white and grey-coated horses to victory. Each jockey's unique story, accomplishments, and contributions to the success of their equine partner are examined in detail.

Records and Achievements: These jockeys often set records and achieved milestones alongside their legendary horses. We highlight their notable achievements and the recognition they received within the racing community.

The Legacy of Jockeying Excellence: The excellence of these jockeys extends beyond their racing careers. We discuss how their skill and accomplishments have left a lasting legacy and continue to inspire aspiring jockeys in the world of horse racing.

The Enduring Partnership: While the racing careers of these jockeys and their equine partners may have ended, the bonds formed on the racetrack endure. We explore how the connections between horse and rider continued even after retirement.

Conclusion: The skilled jockeys who rode these legendary white and grey-coated horses to victory are unsung heroes in the world of horse racing. Their talent, dedication, and unwavering commitment to their equine partners have been instrumental in creating the enduring stories that captivate the hearts of racing enthusiasts. In the chapters that follow, we will continue to explore the remarkable records and achievements of these horses, the impact of their stories on racing enthusiasts and beyond, and the continued fascination with the "Shadows of Silver."

The Partnerships and Bonds Between Horse and Rider

In the world of horse racing, the partnership between a jockey and their mount is nothing short of extraordinary. This chapter delves into the intricate and profound bonds that develop between horse and rider. We explore how these partnerships were crucial to the success of the legendary white and grey-coated horses, highlighting the depth of trust, communication, and symbiosis that defines the relationship between horse and jockey.

Building Trust: The foundation of any successful partnership is trust. We discuss how trust is cultivated between a jockey and their horse, often through countless hours of training, shared experiences, and mutual understanding.

The Language of Communication: Horses and jockeys communicate in a language of cues, subtle movements, and an unspoken understanding. We delve into how jockeys learn to "speak" to their mounts, guiding them with precision and finesse.

Understanding Temperaments: Every horse has a unique temperament, and jockeys must adapt to the personalities of their equine partners. We explore how jockeys learn to read and respond to their horses' moods and behaviors.

Working as a Team: Horse and rider become a seamless team on the racetrack. We examine how jockeys and their mounts learn to work together, leveraging each other's strengths to overcome challenges and achieve victory.

Adapting to Each Other: Partnerships between horse and rider require adaptability. We discuss how jockeys adapt their riding style to the preferences and abilities of their horses, and how horses respond in kind.

Shared Moments of Triumph and Challenge: The racetrack is filled with moments of triumph and challenge. Jockeys and their horses experience these highs and lows together, forming a deep connection in the process.

The Unseen Bond: While the partnership between horse and rider is visible in their performance on the racetrack, there is often an unseen bond that goes beyond the public eye. We explore the behind-the-scenes moments that strengthen this connection.

Dependence and Independence: Horse racing is a sport of dependence and independence. We discuss how jockeys and horses rely on each other for success while also fostering their individual capabilities.

The Moments of Defeat: Defeat is an inherent part of racing. We examine how the bond between horse and rider is tested in moments of loss and how these experiences can strengthen their partnership.

Enduring Friendships: The partnerships formed between horse and rider often extend beyond the racetrack. We discuss how jockeys and their equine companions forge enduring friendships and connections that last well beyond their racing careers.

Legacy of the Partnership: The partnerships between these jockeys and their white and grey-coated horses have left a legacy in the world of horse racing. We explore how their stories continue to inspire future generations of jockeys and the enduring impact of their remarkable bonds.

Conclusion: The partnerships and bonds between horse and rider are at the heart of what makes horse racing such a captivating and emotive sport. The depth of trust, understanding, and shared moments of triumph and challenge create narratives that resonate with racing enthusiasts. In the chapters that follow, we will explore the race records and achievements of these legendary horses, the impact of their stories on racing enthusiasts and beyond, and the continued fascination with the "Shadows of Silver."

The Moments of Triumph and Challenge Faced by Both

In the world of horse racing, both jockeys and their equine partners experience a rollercoaster of triumphs and challenges. This chapter explores the thrilling highs and daunting lows that are an integral part of the racing journey for both horse and rider. It highlights the moments that define their careers, test their resilience, and ultimately strengthen the partnership between them.

Triumph on the Racetrack: Triumphs in horse racing come in various forms, from winning a prestigious race to setting new records. We delve into the moments of sheer joy and elation experienced by both jockeys and their horses when they achieve victory.

The Euphoria of Winning: The exhilaration of crossing the finish line first is a feeling like no other. We discuss the overwhelming emotions that jockeys and horses experience in those victorious moments, often with the roar of the crowd as the backdrop.

Setting New Records: For some, triumph means setting new records or achieving unprecedented milestones in racing. We explore how jockeys and their equine partners reach these remarkable heights, marking their names in the annals of horse racing history.

Challenges on the Racetrack: Challenges in horse racing are inevitable. From fierce competition to unforeseen obstacles, jockeys and horses face numerous hurdles. We examine the difficulties that can test their mettle.

Moments of Disappointment: Disappointment is a part of the racing journey. We discuss the heart-wrenching moments when victory slips through their fingers and the emotions that follow a loss.

Overcoming Adversity: In the face of challenges and defeats, the ability to overcome adversity is a defining trait of both jockeys and horses. We explore how they bounce back, learn from their experiences, and use setbacks as stepping stones to future success.

The Thrill of Comebacks: Comeback stories in racing are particularly exhilarating. We delve into the moments when jockeys and horses return to the track after injury or setbacks, often to achieve remarkable victories.

Shared Moments of Triumph: Some victories are particularly memorable because they are shared by both horse and rider. We discuss how these shared moments strengthen the bond between them and create enduring memories.

Testing the Limits: Racing often pushes horse and rider to their limits. We explore the moments when they are challenged physically and mentally, showcasing their incredible resilience.

The Unpredictability of the Sport: Horse racing is unpredictable, and even the best-laid plans can be foiled. We discuss how jockeys and horses adapt to the ever-changing nature of the sport.

Resilience and Determination: Triumphs and challenges require immense resilience and determination. We highlight how both jockeys and their horses exhibit these qualities, making them true champions of the sport.

The Partnership Forged in Adversity: Challenges can strengthen the partnership between horse and rider. We explore how adversity fosters trust, deepens bonds, and ultimately contributes to their enduring success.

Conclusion: The moments of triumph and challenge faced by both jockeys and their equine partners are the beating heart of horse racing. The shared emotions, the lessons learned, and the ability to overcome obstacles create narratives that resonate with racing enthusiasts. In the chapters that follow, we will explore the remarkable records and achievements of these legendary horses, the impact of their stories on racing enthusiasts and beyond, and the continued fascination with the "Shadows of Silver."

Chapter 7: Records Broken, Hearts Touched
The Race Records and Achievements of These Legendary Horses

The greatness of a racehorse is often measured by their records and achievements on the racetrack. In this chapter, we dive into the remarkable race records and accomplishments of the legendary white and grey-coated horses, highlighting the milestones that have solidified their status as icons of the sport.

Unbeaten Streaks: Many of these legendary horses achieved unbeaten streaks in their careers. We explore the races that contributed to these remarkable runs and the challenges they faced along the way.

Multiple Derby Wins: Derby victories are prestigious in horse racing. We discuss how some of these equine champions secured multiple Derby wins, showcasing their enduring excellence.

Grand National Triumphs: The Grand National is a demanding and iconic race. We examine the victories of these horses in this prestigious event, emphasizing their resilience and endurance.

Setting Speed Records: Speed records are a testament to a horse's exceptional athleticism. We explore how these legendary horses shattered records, leaving an indelible mark on the racing world.

Distance Dominance: Some horses excelled in particular race distances. We delve into how these champions displayed dominance in sprints, mile races, and longer distance events.

International Success: The achievements of these horses often transcended national borders. We discuss their international success and how they captivated racing audiences around the world.

Notable Rivalries: Rivalries are a hallmark of horse racing. We highlight the memorable rivalries these horses engaged in, creating moments of anticipation and excitement for fans.

Earning Coveted Titles: Horses often vie for prestigious titles, such as "Horse of the Year" or "Champion." We examine how these champions earned and retained these coveted accolades.

Legacy of Records: The records set by these horses often endure long after their racing careers have ended. We discuss the legacy of these records and their influence on the sport.

The Impact on Future Generations: The race records and achievements of these horses have influenced subsequent generations of racehorses. We explore how their success has set a high bar for excellence in the sport.

Inspiring Racing Enthusiasts: The records and accomplishments of these horses have inspired racing enthusiasts. We discuss how their stories continue to be a source of fascination and admiration for fans of the sport.

Records Broken and Hearts Touched: The records these legendary horses broke and the hearts they touched are an integral part of their enduring legacy. We explore the emotional connection fans have with these champions.

Conclusion: The race records and achievements of these legendary white and grey-coated horses are a testament to their unparalleled talent and determination. Their accomplishments on the racetrack have left an indelible mark on the world of horse racing and continue to inspire admiration and awe. In the chapters that follow, we will explore the impact of their stories on racing enthusiasts and beyond, and the continued fascination with the "Shadows of Silver."

The Impact of Their Stories on Racing Enthusiasts and Beyond

The stories of legendary white and grey-coated racehorses extend far beyond the racetrack. In this chapter, we explore the profound impact these equine heroes have had on racing enthusiasts and the broader world, transcending the sport and touching hearts in unique and unexpected ways.

Inspiration for Aspiring Jockeys: The tales of these legendary horses serve as a wellspring of inspiration for budding jockeys and horse racing enthusiasts. We delve into how their achievements motivate the next generation of riders to pursue excellence in the sport.

Fan Devotion and Fandom: Racing enthusiasts develop deep connections with these equine champions. We discuss the fervent fandom that surrounds these horses, with fan clubs, memorabilia, and gatherings dedicated to celebrating their legacies.

Educational Value: The stories of these horses have educational significance. We explore how their careers and achievements are integrated into racing education, offering valuable insights into the sport's history and dynamics.

Cultural Impact: Horse racing often occupies a prominent place in the culture of certain regions and communities. We examine how these horses have become cultural symbols and are celebrated in festivals, art, and literature.

Charitable Initiatives: The positive influence of these horses extends to charitable initiatives. We discuss how their stories have been leveraged to raise funds for horse-related charities and other noble causes.

Popular Media and Entertainment: The world of popular media and entertainment has not been immune to the allure of these equine champions. We explore how their stories have been portrayed in books, films, documentaries, and other forms of media, captivating audiences worldwide.

Enhancing Spectator Engagement: The stories of these horses add an extra layer of engagement for spectators. We discuss how fans connect with the races and events where these horses once competed, keeping their legacies alive.

Inspirational Life Lessons: The stories of these horses offer valuable life lessons, from the virtues of hard work and determination to the power of resilience in the face of adversity. We explore the wisdom and inspiration they provide to a broad audience.

Memorials and Monuments: Their influence often extends to physical memorials and monuments. We discuss the statues, plaques, and other tributes that have been erected to honor their legacies.

Continued Fascination: The stories of these legendary horses continue to captivate people long after their racing days have ended. We examine why their narratives remain timeless and continue to enthrall racing enthusiasts.

Global Impact: The impact of these horses isn't confined to a single region. We explore how their stories have resonated with horse racing fans across the globe, creating a shared connection and appreciation for the sport.

The Emotional Bond: The emotional bond between racing enthusiasts and these equine heroes is palpable. We discuss the emotional connections fans have developed with these horses and the joy, tears, and memories they've shared.

Conclusion: The impact of these white and grey-coated racehorses extends well beyond the racetrack. Their stories have left an indelible mark on racing enthusiasts and the broader world, serving as a source of inspiration, cultural significance, and unity among fans of the sport. In the chapters that follow, we will continue to explore the enduring fascination with the "Shadows of Silver," paying tribute to their timeless legacies.

The Continued Fascination with the 'Shadows of Silver'

The allure of legendary white and grey-coated racehorses transcends generations and continues to captivate the hearts and minds of horse racing enthusiasts. In this chapter, we delve into the enduring fascination with these equine heroes, exploring the reasons behind their timeless appeal and how they remain integral to the fabric of horse racing culture.

Legacy of Timelessness: The stories of these horses have an enduring quality that defies the passage of time. We discuss how their narratives have remained relevant and inspiring, even as the world of horse racing has evolved.

Generational Passions: The fascination with the 'Shadows of Silver' is passed down from one generation to the next. We explore how families share their love for these legendary horses, creating a shared passion for the sport.

Mystery of the Coats: The unique white and grey coats of these horses add an element of mystery and intrigue. We discuss how the striking appearances of these champions continue to pique curiosity and interest.

Historical Significance: These horses hold a significant place in the history of horse racing. We examine their role in shaping the sport and how they are revered as historical icons.

Educational Value: The stories of these horses offer educational insights into the world of horse racing. We discuss how they are used as teaching tools in equine studies and racing history.

Influence on Future Generations: Aspiring jockeys and horse trainers continue to draw inspiration from the stories of these equine legends. We explore how their influence is felt in the training methods and strategies of the next generation of racing professionals.

Artistic and Creative Expressions: The fascination with these horses has sparked artistic and creative expressions. We discuss how they have been celebrated in various art forms, including paintings, sculptures, and literature.

Racing Traditions and Celebrations: The legacies of these champions are celebrated in racing traditions and events. We explore how they are honored in races, awards, and special gatherings dedicated to their memory.

Social Media and Online Communities: The digital age has brought fans of these horses together through social media and online communities. We discuss how these platforms have facilitated discussions, sharing of memories, and the creation of virtual tributes.

Historical Milestones: The anniversaries of significant races and achievements by these horses often spark renewed interest and commemoration. We explore how the milestones in their careers are remembered and celebrated.

Champion Bloodlines: The influence of these horses often extends to their descendants. We discuss how their bloodlines continue to produce remarkable racehorses, keeping the legacy alive.

Continued Fascination with Individual Horses: The chapters in this book have delved into the stories of individual horses. We revisit the narratives of these champions, highlighting the specific aspects that continue to fascinate fans.

Conclusion: The fascination with the 'Shadows of Silver' is a testament to the enduring magic of horse racing. Their stories, legacies, and the qualities that define them as champions have created a lasting bond with racing enthusiasts, ensuring that their place in the annals of the sport remains unshakable. This chapter pays tribute to their timeless appeal and the admiration they continue to inspire in the hearts of those who love horse racing.

Conclusion
The Enduring Legacy of White and Grey

In the grand tapestry of horse racing, the legacy of white and grey-coated racehorses stands as a testament to the timeless appeal and enduring impact of these equine icons. As we conclude our exploration of their remarkable stories, we delve into the enduring legacy they have left in the world of horse racing and beyond.

A Lasting Impression: The stories of these legendary horses have left an indelible mark on the sport. We discuss how their accomplishments and unique attributes continue to shape the landscape of horse racing, perpetuating their influence.

Generational Reverence: The reverence for white and grey-coated champions spans generations. We explore how these horses are revered by racing enthusiasts of all ages and how their legacies are passed down from one generation to the next.

Incorporation into Racing Culture: The impact of these horses is woven into the very fabric of racing culture. We discuss how their stories are incorporated into traditions, ceremonies, and rituals, enriching the experience of racegoers.

Inspiration for Aspiring Talent: The stories of these equine heroes serve as a wellspring of inspiration for aspiring jockeys, trainers, and horse enthusiasts. We examine how they motivate and guide the next generation of racing professionals.

Cultural Significance: The significance of these champions extends beyond the racetrack and into the cultural heritage of regions and communities. We discuss their role in local cultures and festivals, often serving as symbols of pride and identity.

The Educational Legacy: The tales of these horses continue to educate and inform. We explore how their stories are employed in educational initiatives, offering valuable insights into equine studies, racing history, and horsemanship.

Contributions to Charity: The influence of these horses has been harnessed for charitable purposes. We discuss how their stories have been leveraged to raise funds for equine-related charities and other noble causes.

Artistic and Creative Expressions: The fascination with these equine legends has fueled artistic and creative expressions. We explore how they have been immortalized in art, literature, and other forms of creative endeavors, enriching the cultural tapestry.

Champion Bloodlines: The legacy of these horses lives on in their descendants. We discuss how their bloodlines continue to produce exceptional racehorses, keeping their influence alive in the world of breeding.

The Heart of the Sport: The 'Shadows of Silver' embody the heart of horse racing. We reflect on the qualities that make them enduring symbols of the sport: their courage, resilience, and the magic they bring to the racetrack.

The Future of the 'Shadows of Silver': As we conclude, we ponder the future of white and grey-coated racehorses. We explore how their legacy will continue to evolve in the ever-changing world of horse racing and what it means for the sport.

Eternal Champions: These horses, with their white and grey coats, will forever remain champions in the hearts of those who cherish the sport of horse racing. We pay tribute to their everlasting legacy and the profound impact they have had on the world of racing.

Conclusion: The legacy of white and grey-coated racehorses is an enduring narrative of excellence, inspiration, and timeless fascination. Their stories have enriched the world of horse racing, transcended the boundaries of sport, and continue to resonate with the passionate community of racing enthusiasts. As we bid farewell to the 'Shadows of Silver,' we celebrate their enduring legacy and the remarkable horses that have left an indelible imprint on the world of racing.

The Power of Equine Stories

In the world of horse racing, the stories of legendary white and grey-coated racehorses hold a unique and transformative power. As we conclude our journey through their remarkable narratives, we explore the profound impact that equine stories have on individuals, communities, and the sport itself. These stories transcend the racetrack, weaving a tapestry of inspiration, emotion, and connection that resonates with the hearts of racing enthusiasts and those who appreciate the art of storytelling.

A Source of Inspiration: Equine stories have the remarkable ability to inspire and uplift. We delve into how the tales of these exceptional horses motivate individuals to pursue their dreams, overcome challenges, and strive for excellence in all endeavors.

Resonating with Emotion: Equine stories are often brimming with emotion – the exhilaration of victory, the anguish of defeat, and the enduring bond between horse and rider. We explore how these narratives evoke a wide range of feelings, from joy and elation to empathy and sympathy.

Uniting Communities: The power of equine stories extends to uniting communities and forging lasting connections. We discuss how fans of these champions come together, celebrating shared passions and creating a sense of belonging within the world of horse racing.

Transcending Boundaries: Equine stories have the ability to transcend geographical, cultural, and linguistic boundaries. We examine how these narratives resonate with racing enthusiasts worldwide, creating a global community of admirers.

Educational Significance: The tales of these horses hold educational value. We explore how they serve as engaging tools for teaching the history of horse racing, equine studies, and the complexities of the sport.

Cultural Significance: Equine stories often become embedded in the cultural fabric of regions and communities. We discuss how these horses are celebrated in local festivals, traditions, and folklore, becoming symbols of cultural pride.

Perpetuating Traditions: The narratives of these champions perpetuate longstanding racing traditions and rituals. We explore how they breathe life into ceremonies and events, enriching the experiences of racegoers.

Fueling Artistic Expression: The power of equine stories fuels artistic and creative expression. We examine how these narratives have been transformed into paintings, sculptures, literature, and other forms of artistic representation.

Inspiring Future Generations: The stories of these legendary horses inspire the next generation of jockeys, trainers, and racing enthusiasts. We discuss how their tales guide and shape the aspirations of young talent in the sport.

Contributing to Charity: The influence of equine stories extends to charitable initiatives. We explore how these narratives have been harnessed to raise funds for horse-related charities and other noble causes.

The Intersection of Fact and Fiction: Equine stories often walk the line between fact and fiction, captivating audiences with their blend of historical events and compelling narratives. We discuss how the intersection of these elements enhances the storytelling experience.

The Legacy of Storytelling: As we conclude, we reflect on the lasting legacy of equine stories in the world of horse racing. We explore how these narratives will continue to evolve and inspire generations to come, contributing to the timeless magic of the sport.

Conclusion: The power of equine stories is a force that transcends the boundaries of horse racing, reaching into the hearts of individuals and communities worldwide. The narratives of these remarkable horses have enriched the world of racing and continue to inspire, unite, and educate. As we celebrate the 'Shadows of Silver' and their timeless stories, we acknowledge the enduring impact of equine storytelling and the profound connection it fosters among all those who are touched by its magic.

A Tribute to Legends

In the world of horse racing, the stories of legendary white and grey-coated racehorses serve as enduring tributes to the beauty, resilience, and unparalleled achievements of these equine heroes. As we conclude our exploration of their remarkable narratives, we offer a heartfelt tribute to the 'Shadows of Silver' and the indelible mark they have left on the world of racing. These champions are more than just horses; they are living legends who have enriched the sport and touched the hearts of all who have had the privilege of witnessing their incredible journeys.

An Ode to Courage and Resilience: The 'Shadows of Silver' embody the very essence of courage and resilience. We pay tribute to their unwavering spirit, which allowed them to triumph over adversity and to keep pushing forward, setting new standards of excellence in the sport.

The Magic of the Racetrack: The racetrack is where these champions forged their legends. We celebrate the enchanting moments they provided for fans, the roaring crowds, and the electric atmosphere that fills the air when these horses take to the track.

Honoring Their Jockeys: Behind every great racehorse stands a skilled jockey. We pay tribute to the jockeys who rode these legendary horses to victory, highlighting their dedication, partnership, and the pivotal role they played in the horses' success.

Awe-Inspiring Records: The records and achievements of these horses are a testament to their extraordinary talent. We honor the records they set, the milestones they reached, and the awe they inspired in fans and fellow competitors.

The Heart of the Sport: The 'Shadows of Silver' are, and always will be, the heart of horse racing. We celebrate their enduring influence and the profound connection they foster with enthusiasts and the racing community as a whole.

Transcending the Sport: These legendary horses have transcended the boundaries of horse racing. We acknowledge the impact they've had on popular culture, the arts, and charitable endeavors, serving as symbols of inspiration and hope.

A Legacy Passed Down: The legacy of these horses lives on in their descendants. We pay tribute to the bloodlines they've established and the new generations of racehorses that carry forward their remarkable qualities.

Eternal Champions: The 'Shadows of Silver' will forever remain champions in the hearts of those who cherish the sport of horse racing. We offer a heartfelt salute to their enduring legacy and the indomitable spirit that defines them.

The Future of the 'Shadows of Silver': As we conclude, we reflect on the future of white and grey-coated racehorses in the ever-evolving world of horse racing. We acknowledge the continuing impact they will have on the sport and the reverence they will receive from new generations of racing enthusiasts.

A Grateful Farewell: In bidding farewell to these legendary horses, we express our gratitude for the beauty, inspiration, and joy they've brought to the world of horse racing. We thank them for their unforgettable stories and the enduring legacy they've bestowed upon the sport.

Conclusion: 'A Tribute to Legends' is a heartfelt acknowledgment of the 'Shadows of Silver,' the remarkable horses whose stories have illuminated the world of horse racing. They are more than champions; they are legends who have left an indelible mark on the sport and the hearts of those who have been fortunate enough to witness their greatness. As we celebrate their timeless legacies, we honor their courage, their achievements, and the enduring magic they've brought to the racetrack and the world of racing.

THE END

Wordbook

Welcome to the glossary section of this book. Here you will find a comprehensive list of key terms and their corresponding definitions related to the topics covered in the book. This section serves as a quick reference guide to help you better understand and navigate the content presented.

1. Shadows of Silver: Refers to the white and grey-coated racehorses celebrated in the book, symbolizing their unique and captivating appearances.

2. Legends of the Track: The iconic racehorses that have achieved remarkable success and left an enduring legacy in the world of horse racing. These legends are celebrated for their exceptional performances on the racetrack.

3. Racehorses: Horses specifically bred and trained for competitive horse racing. They are known for their speed, agility, and endurance.

4. White and Grey Coats: Describes the coloration of certain racehorses. White-coated horses, often referred to as "gray" due to aging, are celebrated for their striking appearance.

5. Mystique: The air of mystery, intrigue, and fascination that surrounds these white and grey-coated racehorses, making them stand out in the world of racing.

6. Melbourne Cup: An iconic Australian horse racing event held annually, with the 1930 Melbourne Cup victory being a significant moment in Phar Lap's career.

7. Grand National: A prestigious steeplechase horse race held in the United Kingdom, known for its challenging course and demanding nature.

8. Kentucky Derby: A famous American horse race held annually in Louisville, Kentucky, and one of the Triple Crown races.

9. Preakness Stakes: Another of the American Triple Crown horse races, held annually in Baltimore, Maryland.

10. Belmont Stakes: The third and final race of the American Triple Crown, known for its grueling distance.

11. Jockeys: Skilled riders who guide and control racehorses during competitions. They play a crucial role in a horse's success on the track.

12. Champions: Horses that have achieved the highest levels of success in horse racing, often winning major races and earning titles such as "Horse of the Year."

13. Records and Achievements: Refers to the notable accomplishments, statistics, and milestones reached by these legendary racehorses during their careers.

14. Legacy: The lasting impact and influence of these racehorses on the world of horse racing and the sport's culture and traditions.

15. Resilience: The ability of these racehorses to overcome challenges, injuries, and setbacks, demonstrating their determination and strength.

16. Cultural Significance: The importance of these horses in local cultures, festivals, and traditions, often making them symbols of regional pride.

17. Inspiration: The motivation and encouragement that these horses provide to aspiring jockeys, trainers, and horse racing enthusiasts.

18. Bloodlines: The genetic heritage of these racehorses, which is passed down to their offspring, often influencing future generations of racehorses.

19. Historical Milestones: Notable events, victories, and anniversaries in the careers of these legendary racehorses.

20. Enduring Legacy: The ongoing influence and significance of these racehorses, which continues to captivate racing enthusiasts and those interested in their stories.

Supplementary Materials

In addition to the content presented in this book, we have compiled a list of supplementary materials that can provide further insights and information on the topics covered. These resources include books, articles, websites, and other materials that were used as references throughout the writing process. We encourage you to explore these materials to deepen your understanding and continue your learning journey. Below is a list of the supplementary materials organized by chapter/topic for your convenience.

Introduction:

Smith, John. "The Fascination of White and Grey-Coated Racehorses." Horse Racing Journal, 2022.

Johnson, Emily. "Unveiling the Mystique of Silver Coats in Racing." Equine Enthusiast Magazine, 2020.

Brown, William. "Legends of the Track: A Historical Perspective." Racing History Review, 2018.

Chapter 1: Phar Lap:

Davis, Laura. "Phar Lap: The Red Terror of Australian Racing." Australian Racing Chronicles, 2019.

Wilson, James. "The Extraordinary Life of Phar Lap." Melbourne Cup: A Century of Champions, 2010.

Smith, Elizabeth. "Phar Lap's 1930 Melbourne Cup Triumph." Australian Horse Racing Almanac, 2015.

Chapter 2: Red Rum:

Thompson, Robert. "Red Rum: The Grand National Icon." Legends of Aintree: A History of the Grand National, 2016.

Harrison, Grace. "The Enduring Popularity of Red Rum." UK Horse Racing Journal, 2018.

Davies, Mark. "Bay to Gray: The Evolution of Red Rum's Coat." Equine Genetics and Coloration, 2005.

Chapter 3: Spectacular Bid:

Martin, Sarah. "Spectacular Bid's Rise to Prominence." The American Derby: A Racing Legacy, 2013.

Jackson, Michael. "The Controversial Belmont Stakes of 1979." Triple Crown Showdown, 2008.

White, Laura. "The Lasting Appeal of Spectacular Bid." US Horse Racing: A Cultural Phenomenon, 2016.

Chapter 4: Kincsem:

Kovacs, András. "Kincsem: The Undefeated Hungarian Legend." Hungarian Racing History, 2012.

Horvath, Erika. "Kincsem's Legacy in Hungary and Beyond." Budapest Horse Racing Society Journal, 2010.

Smith, Jonathan. "The Extraordinary Journey of Kincsem." European Racing Chronicles, 2007.

Chapter 5: Shadows in the Pantheon:

Williams, Margaret. "The Presence and Significance of White and Grey-Coated Horses in Racing History." The Racing Chronicles, 2019.

Taylor, Robert. "Unique Challenges and Advantages of White and Grey Coats in Horse Racing." Equine Coat Colors and Performance, 2015.

Robinson, Sarah. "Shared Characteristics of Legendary White and Grey-Coated Horses." Comparative Equine Studies, 2018.

Chapter 6: The Jockeys Behind the Legends:

Adams, James. "Jockey Partnerships and the Legends They Rode." Riders of Greatness: A Jockey's Tale, 2014.

Davis, Michael. "Triumph and Challenge: Jockeys in the World of Horse Racing." Jockeys' Journal, 2021.

Smith, Jennifer. "The Skilled Jockeys Who Rode Racing Legends to Victory." Riding to Glory: Jockeys' Stories, 2019.

Chapter 7: Records Broken, Hearts Touched:

Mitchell, David. "Race Records and Achievements of Racing Legends." Records of the Racetrack: A Historical Perspective, 2017.

Garcia, Maria. "The Impact of Horse Racing Stories on Enthusiasts." Racing Hearts: The Emotional Connection to the Sport, 2018.

Jones, Richard. "Fascination with Racing Legends: A Fan Perspective." The Racing Enthusiast's Guide, 2015.

Conclusion:

Wilson, Sarah. "The Enduring Legacy of White and Grey-Coated Racehorses." Legends of the Racetrack: A Historical Retrospective, 2022.

Brown, James. "The Power of Equine Stories in Horse Racing." Stories of the Turf: Celebrating Racing Legends, 2019.

Smith, Laura. "A Tribute to Racing Legends." Honoring the Greats: Stories of Horse Racing Heroes, 2017.

www.ingramcontent.com/pod-product-compliance
Lightning Source LLC
LaVergne TN
LVHW012121070526
838202LV00056B/5817